SAINT GUINEFORT

PROTECTOR OF CHILDREN

SINCE THE THIRTEENTH CENTURY

By Gary K. Sturni and George G. Mellios
Illustrations by Logan B. Walker

This book belongs to

_____

_____

A portion of the proceeds from this book will be used for international aid for children.

It is often said that if dogs don't go to heaven, I'm not sure that I want to go there either. With the story of Guinefort, we have an opportunity to rejoice that God has obviously sent dogs from heaven to be among us with saintly love and devotion. Certainly my dogs, Ruth and Naomi, would agree.

The Rt. Rev. Don E. Johnson, Episcopal Bishop of West Tennessee

The unique Christian legend of the loyal dog Guinefort is now retold by Father Sturni and George Mellios with both care and an energetic pace. This story is further enhanced with clear and boldly colored illustrations by Logan Walker. The result is a modern recreation of a children's Mediaeval illuminated "passional" or a recounting of the life of a saint. - *E. A. Carmean, Jr., Art Historian and Cultural Essayist*

"Dear Dr. Sturni: I am looking for an icon of St. Guinefort for my private chapel. And, note, no dog is mere child's play. Dogs may be humankind's greatest contribution to the world." *The Rev'd J. Timothy West*

Dedicated to our grandchildren, and grandchildren yet to come:

Rori MacKenzie

Hattie Patenaude

Ruth Sturni

Jordan Watkins

Vaughn Archer

Jack Archer

James Archer

and to another loyal and loving dog, Bella.

Authors' Note: The authors hold the cult of saints of the Roman Catholic, Orthodox and Anglican traditions in high respect. Recounting the lore of St. Guinefort is to tell yet another story about a noble dog, the kind of tale that perennially delights children, parents (and grandparents). The fact that Guinefort was so loved as to have been proclaimed a saint is a whimsical testimony to the attachment we have to our pets. (It was shortly after this that Rome promulgated official guidelines about who could become a saint; see Catherine Bilow's Note to Parents on the back page.)

The violent battle with a snake and the cruel injustice of Guinefort's banishment are story elements no worse than appear in the Brothers Grimm. Bruno Bettelheim, in *The Uses of Enchantment,* points out that children understand that bad things happen to good people, and that this then leads to a heightened anticipation of a moral victory and exultation of goodness, which concludes this and other such stories. (Still, it took two of us pondering long to adapt the original story to a version appropriate for children.)

Those wishing to know more about the origins of Guinefort's story may find Jean-Claude Schmitt's *The Holy Greyhound: Guinefort, Healer of Children since the Thirteenth Century* (Cambridge University Press, Paris, 1983) of great interest. GKS

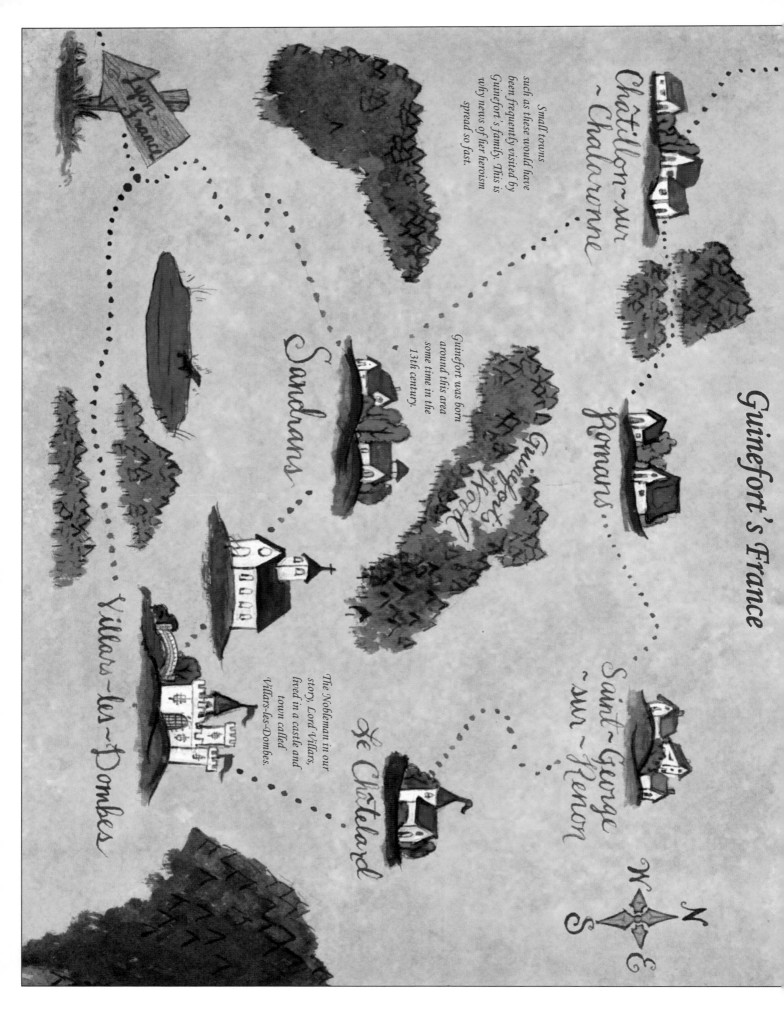

Guinefort's France

Chatillon~sur
~Chalaronne

Small towns
such as these would have
been frequently visited by
Guinefort's family. This is
why news of her heroism
spread so fast.

Lyon, France

Sandrans

Guinefort was born
around this area
some time in the
13th century.

Guinefort's Forest

Romans

Saint~George
~sur~Renon

Villars~les~Dombes

Le Châtelard

The Nobleman in our
story, Lord Villars,
lived in a castle and
town called
Villars-les-Dombes.

N W S E

ong ago in the beautiful French countryside near Lyons, a Greyhound puppy was born. Her father's name was Napoleon, and her mother's name was Katherine. Napoleon was fast, strong, and brave. His tan color looked like shiny gold in the sun. Her mother was white with tan patches and very pretty. She was loving, kind, and gentle.

Their new puppy was bright white, and oh so cute. They were very proud of their beautiful new baby girl, Guinefort.

They lived in the country and had lots of fun playing together in the park where there were many things to see and do. They would run, watch the squirrels and rabbits and play with the town children. They were such friendly dogs that people came from far away to watch them play with each other and with the children in the park.

As Guinefort grew up, it was clear she was special: she could tell the difference between right and wrong and good and bad. Guinefort would protect smaller dogs from bullies.

When children were playing together happily, she smiled and wagged her tail and glowed with happiness.

Guinefort's family became known throughout all France, and caught the attention of a nobleman and his wife who were searching for a trustworthy dog to watch over their newborn baby. He traveled across the kingdom to see for himself the dog family he had heard so much about.

When he arrived at the park, he was impressed to see how much the other dogs and people of the town really liked Guinefort and her parents. He could see that Guinefort played with the children, kept them safe, and made them happy.

When the nobleman met Guinefort, he and
she immediately liked each other.

Having become good friends with the nobleman so quickly, and because she was getting older, Guinefort excitedly asked her parents if she could go live with the nobleman's family and be a companion to their child. They said "Yes." The nobleman was overjoyed that Guinefort was coming to their home. He invited Napoleon and Catherine to visit at any time.

When the baby was sleeping, Guinefort would lie on the floor and rest right beside him in the crib, watching his every breath to be sure he was safe. One day, Bishop Édouard dropped by to visit the family and saw Guinefort playing with the baby. When the baby was awake, Guinefort would toss her toys up in the air and catch them.

This made the baby laugh and clap his hands with delight. Sometimes when the baby was grumpy or was not feeling well, it was hard even for his parents to comfort him. But Guinefort could always cheer the baby up and make him feel better. Guinefort made sure that the baby was always happy and safe.

Guinefort and the baby loved each other so much that the nobleman would invite his friends to watch them play, do tricks and have fun. Everyone was amazed that a dog and baby were such good friends. The Bishop especially loved how Guinefort and the baby played together.

Guinefort went everywhere with the nobleman's family. They would have picnics, baby carriage rides, and walks through the park. Every Sunday they all went to church.

The Bishop gave Guinefort her own cushion to sit on during the service. Guinefort was so good in church and with the baby that the Bishop thought she was blessed with divine goodness!

One day while the baby was napping, an evil snake crept into the room where the baby was fast asleep. The snake was ever so quiet as it slithered towards the baby!

But Guinefort heard a noise as it climbed towards the baby's crib. She rushed toward the crib, grabbed the snake and shook it, and broke off its tail.

There was a lot of noise and a terrible mess! The injured snake, now defeated, quickly retreated to the place from which it had come.

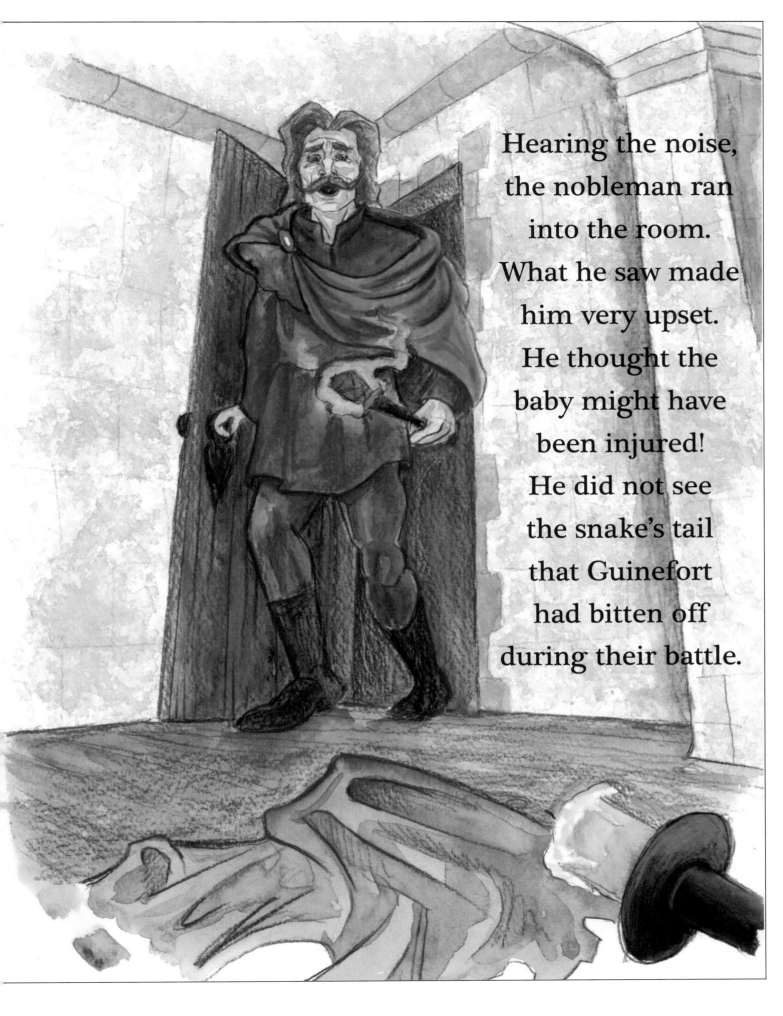

Hearing the noise, the nobleman ran into the room. What he saw made him very upset. He thought the baby might have been injured! He did not see the snake's tail that Guinefort had bitten off during their battle.

He thought Guinefort had hurt the baby and made the mess all by herself. He was so angry that he told Guinefort to leave the house … and never come back!

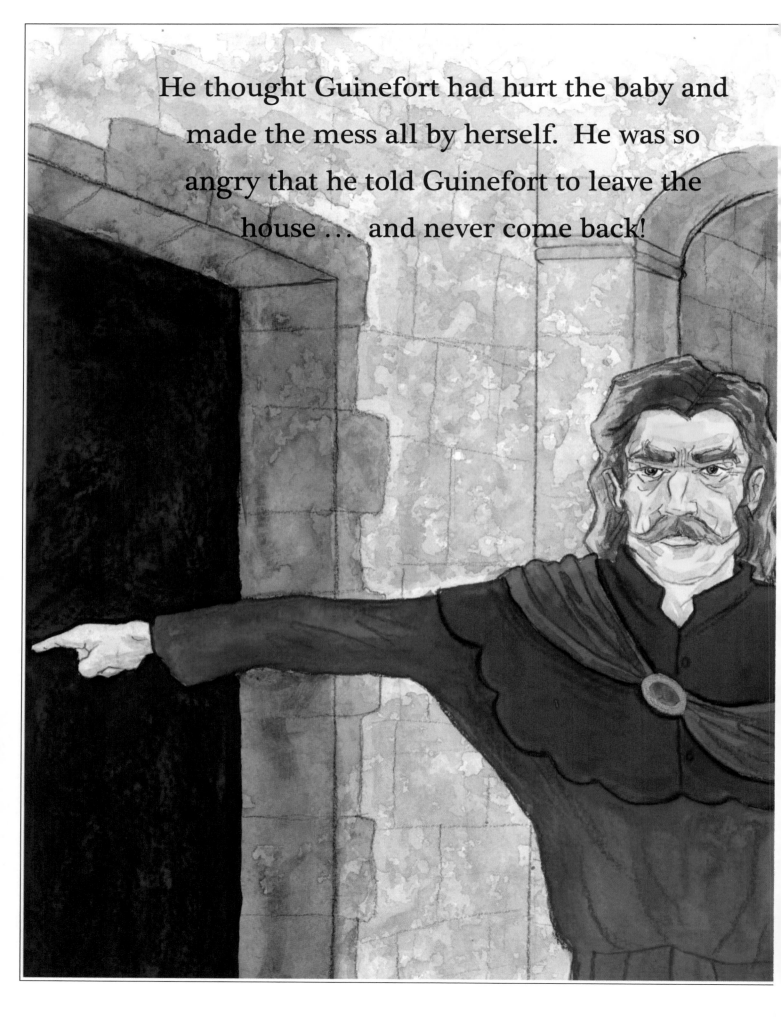

Guinefort knew she had done nothing wrong.
Her feelings were very hurt, and she was very scared
and sad. But she obeyed her master, and left…
never to return in this life.

After Guinefort had been sent away, the nobleman looked around the room again and saw that his baby was unharmed. Then he found bits of snakeskin and the snake's tail Guinefort had bitten off during their fight. He realized he had made a terrible mistake. Guine-fort had been bravely protecting the baby!

For weeks the nobleman asked forgiveness from God for treating Guinefort so badly. But one night —perhaps in a dream — he saw a bright glow coming from the baby's room. He stood up, went over to the door, and looked in.

It was Guinefort! She was sitting by the crib in the nursery and was surrounded by angels! Even after the nobleman had been so mean to Guinefort, the loyal dog came back to protect the baby.

The nobleman was so amazed by what he had seen he ran to tell the Bishop. Bishop Édouard immediately proclaimed her a saint: "Saint Guinefort, Protector of Children."

Soon everyone was travelling to the Nobleman's house to ask St. Guinefort to watch over their children too.

The story of Saint Guinefort reminds us that God loves us as much as we love our pets — and more! Our Guardian Angel prays to God for our protection and safety — and when our pet wags her tale and gives us a kiss, we feel better — and closer to God!

A COLLECT FOR ST. GUINEFORT, LOYAL DOG, "PROTECTOR OF CHILDREN"
AUGUST 22

Heavenly Father, through your gifts of imagination and whimsy your people raised up the loyal dog Guinefort to be a saintly sign of your care for children; May we, inspired by the story of her unflagging loyalty, devotion to duty, and humble suffering, stand strong for the protection of children everywhere. Bless all who, like Etienne de Bourbon, work to make you more truly known, and let us, with simple faith as pilgrims, seek to carry your children to places of safety, healing and delight; through Jesus Christ our Lord. Amen.

TO THE PARENTS

If you ever read *Black Beauty* or *The Call of the Wild* as a child, you already know how compelling animal stories can be. English veterinarian James Herriot penned the memoirs of his lengthy career in caring for animals of various sizes and dispositions, with the happy result that the stories eventually made their way from print to a successful BBC series. Animal stories have the potential to inspires their readers and that is the intent of the author of this particular story.

The story itself is not new; the expression is.

The tale of the faithful greyhound developed from the report of a Dominican friar of the thirteenth century. Étienne (Stephen) of Bourbon spent many of his priestly years examining pious beliefs and defending Christianity from abuses. He was, in fact, among the earliest of the Church's Inquisitors. These clerics, representatives of Church authority, were assigned the task of investigating the life and spiritual practices of each curé (parish priest) and his respective congregation. Among the voluminous writings of this friar, entitled *De Septem Donis Spiritus Sancti ("Concerning the Seven Gifts of the Holy Spirit"),* comes a section he entitles *De Supersticione.* And it is in this compilation that the legend of the greyhound named Guinefort is documented.

This faithful canine enjoyed a reputation that waxed long after her mortal life tragically ended. In company with Paul Bunyan and Pecos Bill, the loyal Guinefort grew in merit as her memory was recounted from one generation to the next. And because the memory of her deeds was squarely set in the history of the Middle Ages, it readily became embroidered by embellishments and hampered by distortions. Faith melded with superstition over time and so the historical figure, as so often happened during this time, was lost beneath overlays of cherished tradition and pious village custom. The facts are few but poignant. Quite certainly the dog belonged to a nobleman whose abode was near Lyons in France. The pet's tragic death at the hands of her own master (reportedly Lord Villars in the area of Ain-Lyons-Dombe) came through the owner's mistake. Rather than attacking the family's infant son, the dog actually defended the child from a threatening snake. Filled with remorse over the cruelty of his impulsive reaction, the nobleman buried the greyhound on his property.

The site grew in status from pet grave to pilgrim shrine. It was mothers of sickly children who especially sought relief by visiting the burial site. One can imagine the mothers' progression from praying to God for their children at this place to then praying to Guinefort.

And so began her saintly reputation. She was even assigned a patronal feast day, August 22. This recognition and growing reverence developed before the start of the Church's official process for canonization (the steps leading up to the Church's acknowledgement of sanctity). It was, rather *vox populi, vox Dei.* In other words, the people's sheer faith in the dog's sanctity seemed enough to suppose that God Himself concurred. It was just such pious suppositions that Inquisitors like Étienne of Bourbon were deputed to correct.

Not unlike Paul Bunyan and Pecos Bill, Guinefort enjoys a lengthy afterlife in a larger-than-life reputation. Her prestige is not simply a vestige of medieval folklore. As recently as 1987, Guinefort was introduced to a new generation. Pamela Berger, among the Fine Arts faculty of Boston College, released a film entitled *Le Sorceress,* a retelling of the pious devotion to "Saint" Guinefort among the simple but devout medieval Lyons-area villagers. Lest so distinguished a canine hero slip again into obscurity, Father Gary Sturni, rector of St. George's Episcopal Church (Germantown, TN), and his friend George Mellios, reintroduces Guinefort to today's children. The telling of the story is greatly enhanced by the illustrations of a young parishioner, Logan Walker.

It is hoped that the legend and circumstances of this remarkable character will inspire you and your family. The best news is this: the end of this book is likely not the end of what we know of Guinefort. I have the distinct sense that, for those of you who find this dog particularly appealing, she will return for other adventures.

~ Catherine Bilow, Ph.D.

22201753R00019

Made in the USA
Charleston, SC
12 September 2013